Obliquity

Roland Leach
Obliquity

Acknowledgements

Poems in this collection have been published in *Apeiron Review* (US),
Baby Teeth Journal, *Best Australian Love Poems 2013*,
Best Australian Poetry 2012, *Best Australian Poetry 2015*,
Best Small Fictions 2015 (Queens Ferry Press, US), *Creatrix Anthology 2*,
Imago, *Island*, *Northern Perspective*, *Oblong* (UK), *Poetry* D'Amour *Anthology*,
Prayers of the Secular World, *Regime*, *Rumblefish* (US), *The Moth* (Ireland),
The Weekend Australian, *To End All Wars* (Puncher & Wattman), *Westerly*.

For Susan

Obliquity
ISBN 978 1 76041 796 3
Copyright © text Roland Leach 2019
Cover: Charmaine le Roux

First published 2019 by
GINNINDERRA PRESS
PO Box 3461 Port Adelaide 5015 Australia
www.ginninderrapress.com.au

Contents

Tilt	7
The Cartographer's Sonnet	8
Tidal	9
My Great Aunt	11
Seven Ways of Looking at God	12
Adhesive	14
The Bonesetter	15
Kalahari	17
Parabola	18
To Start a Revolution	19
Before Halley	20
Cook's Last Voyage	21
Iguanas	22
Wreckage	23
Statistically	24
Look! Old People	26
The Film Version of the Poet's Life	27
Eve : ning	28
Perth	29
Font	31
Walled Cities	32
Distance and Mrs Cook	33
Jellyfish	36
Small Detonations	37
Elephants	38
Angle	39
Beachfront	40
Spelling	43
Square of Yellow Light	45
Your Wanderings	46

Chance	47
Avocado	49
Moorings	52
Cows	53
The Bones of a Tiger	54
Age Takes a Socialist	56
Wagtail	57
Finnegan Goes to War	58
Number 7	59
The Five Ages	60
Interstices	63

Tilt

She came to this strip between ocean and loose
sand, hardened smooth, always wet, to think
about obliquity, and how to right her axis
back to that comfortable angle that made
it possible for the seasons, and not
winter and autumn to appear so
frequently. She came to think about
that angle of axis, the twenty-three degrees
that slipped to forty some days. It wasn't
racing kids to ballet or hockey or school,
sorting out dinner, husband and job
that tipped it. It wasn't the things
to be done. More the inconsistencies
inside, that made her run madly happy
one moment, knowing it all worth it,
then that colourless doubt that wasn't sharp or dull,
but shapeless and sticky as raw egg white,
that made her tilt, made her appear leaning
when she was straight, made her aware
of the fragility of being between
solid earth and the fluidity. So she
had to walk the line of coast, feel the edge
where ocean became land, where ocean came
to an end and those who sprang from it
obliged to accept the heavy drag
of gravity that came with walking the earth.

The Cartographer's Sonnet

We woke to find maps of continents, ancient
and unknown, tattooed on our skins. Curved coasts
in sinuate detail, wondrous flourishes
of winds personified. A centaur in one corner,
an angel in the other. We had woken after a night,
a week, a year. Lying on sheets, flailing like waves
beneath us, beaches before us as white
as hallucination. We had woken lost between
longitudes and like light-year travellers
there was no use consulting astrolabes,
measuring stars, going out on deck
and imagining we could resume.
It was morning: after a night, week, year.
We were back from the stars, an island, a room.

Tidal

There is a drama to tides on islands;
islands are dramatic, they are children
wanting attention. There is a carelessness,
something mildly delinquent about them.

Things happen much quicker on islands.
Darwin wrote about islands eloquently,
of the conditions they offer to evolve,
he knew tides could be simply drifts
used to get from one place to another.

On Nusa Lembongan tides can drag you
out to sea in seconds. A tide-shift
that reaches a breaking point, perhaps two
or three hours after high tide; to an untrained

eye it is unnoticeable, a small flicker
of water breaking the surface, but beneath
currents rip and swirl, drives you back into
its past, an earlier delinquent stream.

My mother loved to use the word tide
in all its inflections: the tidal pull
of mornings she would exclaim, or
this perigean tide that has ruled my life.

It must have been when we were at school,
when she was alone, so I imagined
the house filling with water, my mother
dragged from room to room, up passageways,
drying herself before we got home.

Darwin's wife was a devout Christian,
who worried they would not be united
forever because of his heresies. She blamed
the islands, the endless volume of water
surrounding them, its endless movement.

Tropical islands can do that to the mind.
All around the relentless, inevitable
birthings, rampant and visible without shame:
a fecund breeding, a riotous offspring.

Families are not the same despite Tolstoy.
On Nusa Lembongan the islanders
see themselves as family. Villagers
believe in holy days, ceremonies,
join together to dig out a tree, thatch

a roof, yell and scream at cockfights.
Mothers are not dragged around the house,
wives fret less, the old are not abandoned
on atolls, young boys and girls learn the nature
of tides, notice their shifts, the water's light.

My Great Aunt

My great aunt was always looking for a husband.
She had a few and left them all. Attracted to water,
the distance it offered. She was good at loving
from a distance. My great aunt was always looking.
She was a good looker. Took a steamer out of
Liverpool for the islands of the East, imagining
them still as spice islands. Took men of all creed and colour.
Didn't mind a risk my great aunt, could always find
a racetrack. Fell in love with a young naturalist on board,
grey-coated and too occupied with the flight of birds
to notice her. She liked that. Didn't like fawning men.
Just attracted to water and distance.
She had her way though. Lured the poor man
in dresses as soft as butterfly wings, the colour of macaws,
pretending she was in flight, which she was.

Seven Ways of Looking at God

My mother says there are seven ways of looking at God.
She was a mathematician, is still a mathematician,
though the numbers swing from the ecliptic,
as misaligned as young boys. Already she is straying,
staring out the windows at the wagtails,
but now turns back, alert as she has ever been.

Well, first there is the sheer energy cutting
through space as if the universe were thin cloth.
Two: alone in a small boat in the Atlantic.
Of course, there is nothingness
in all its ambiguity mistaken as absence.
I always think of Brahmagupta, writing in Sanskrit,
using zero for the first time, when I think of nothingness.

The memory preoccupies her
and she is looking at the shape of leaves outside,
perhaps thinking that every shape has an equation.
'Mum, what about number four?'
Desire, she says, but falters and continues,
number five is standing on a reef
in a lightning-storm, head back, arms out,
reciting Phlebas the Phoenician.
Ah, she would always include Eliot.

This one I really like, the jellyfish
who never dies – *Turritopsis dohrnii* –
having reproduced, denies maturity
and returns to its youth, dragging back tentacles,
shrivelling to the bottom of the ocean
where it starts again and again.
And seven? She starts with differential calculus but stops:
Seven is an old woman cursed to a nursing home,
waiting for somewhere better to go.

Adhesive

My mother wears a band-aid on her nose
to cover the cancer that's eating
it away. She has worn it for two years
and refuses to see a doctor. We tell
her that it is cancer but she says, No,
I just keep knocking it. Leave me alone.
When my sisters finally bring the doctor
to the house, he tells her it is serious,
it is cancer. It is not, she says. He tells
her again. It will kill you. She looks at him
as if cancer is beneath her. No it won't,
she says. She has been applying band-aids
to the troubles of her life so long
she almost believes they have worked.

The Bonesetter

The bonesetter lays out his instruments,
each bone placed carefully upon the table.
On the flat surface it appears a constellation
of boulders and coastlines, white and arctic.
He starts at the foot. From where all things
will radiate. Phalange, metatarsal, cuneiform…
He is already in love with the naming.

This is just the start. The tibia, fibula.
But the foot is his first child, this is where
he started and is his masterwork.
The network of bones will allow them
to stand straight, to look out one day
over the top of the savannah to see predators.
To dig their feet into the earth and stand.
The seven vertebrae, the hyoid bone
to support the head. All lead to the skull,
offering cranial space for a capacious brain,
this they believe makes them human,
makes them distinct, but it is the foot
that is his opus. An arrangement of bones
that will keep them surefooted, keep that tenuous
hold on earth firm, capable of anything.

There will be man and woman.
The gift of the pelvic bone
must be paid for by the women.
There will be pain in childbirth
but in return women will have strength.

He looks at the bones, now arranged, now
connected on the table. He remembers
each bone and joint cut by hand. Knows someone
who would like to give them a soul, but he's sure
they will invent that for themselves. Instead
he gives them a drop or two of luck
in the joints, knowing this a greater gift.
The foot he returns to. Imagines
the hubris it will breed. Feet firmly placed
in the sand. They will walk across deserts,
step aboard sloping sea decks, step upon
their moon. They will come to believe
it was all created for them, forgetting
that tilt of axis, an obliquity
that can snap bones.

Kalahari

It takes a while to die from a Kalahari
bushman's arrow. Two hours for a steenbok.
Eight for a large buck antelope. Three days
for a giraffe. A slow poison boiled from the *ngwa*
caterpillar to the texture of red jelly.
It is a slow death. Sometimes tribesman track
for days. And it is then. Couched beside
the dying animal they must experience
death. Lay their head against the duiker's side,
its waning pulse. Crying when its cries out,
shuddering when it shakes. You cannot take a life
carelessly. Life is dangerous but not sad.
You must stroke the head of the eland
with the hand that killed it, the dangerous heart.

Parabola

The water must be bubbling with herring
        this morning. Late March and no wind,

the ocean will look polished blue, little or no swell,
        the tide low enough to walk upon.

We used to walk out on the reef, water to
        our knees. You with that old bag slung

across your shoulder so you could unhook
        and slip the fish into.

I would watch you as you cast, watched you
        as you eyed the long parabola

of line move through sky. A white float filled
        loosely with pollard and whale oil.

You watching it till it hit water,
        as if spooled out from your own fingers.

I tried to do the same, but it never
        rose as high, never perfected

that steep arc that seemed the secret to catching
        fish. The long parabola of line

that never seemed to intersect with sky.

To Start a Revolution

To start a revolution, stand in front
of a tank. These days you may tweet
and sms, organise a crowd. Food strikes
once caught the public's eye: refuse to eat,
drink, move. Remember Moses' flight across
the desert was a middle finger raised
against the Pharaoh. Women may refuse
to have sex with partners who support
oppressors. Believe that nothing can
be done without the people's consent,
but be wary. To start a revolution stand
in front of a tank, but be cautious of others
selling it back to you, claiming greater
fuel efficiency and a better range of colours.

Before Halley

It was first depicted woven in wool on linen
in the Bayeux Tapestry, an omen no doubt
of the coming slaughter, the changing of kings.
In the English sky it is a strange sunflower
still attached to its roots, too extraterrestrial
and modern for the Harold beneath, waiting
on his throne, too modern for sullen boats etched
below waiting to cross grave waters, too strange
a light with its burning tail, its equine
tail, like the decorated war horses
on the battlefield. When Giotto paints
his *Nativity* the comet becomes
the Star of Bethlehem leading the Magi
to the stable, the birth of a new king.

Cook's Last Voyage

By today's standards every eighteenth century
sailing ship would have needed a flotilla
of psychologists, therapists, substance-abuse
counsellors and life coaches. Most of the crew
were half-drunk given their daily allowance
of beer and rum, men were regularly flogged
and the strain and stress of storms and scurvy
required commanders who could be trusted
like gods. Cook had been a god but by his last
voyage needed all the therapists that didn't exist.
He was a god struck dumb by lightning:
one moment a man of the Enlightenment,
rational and wise, then the Old Testament
god of vengeance pursuing petty thefts, till
in Kealakekua Bay from his own bickering
he was struck down: no lightning or smoting,
just death by the old human ways of club and dagger.

Iguanas

I sent my father a postcard
        of marine iguanas
                from the Galapagos.

Only time I ever wrote to him.
        He loved goannas
                and lizards.

Loved the way
        they raised their head
                to appraise you.

When he was young
        a racehorse goanna chased him
                and his brothers up a tree.

They would run straight over you
        if you stood still, he said.
                Beautiful animals.

He never said anything
        about the postcard
                until he was in a nursing home.

Those marine iguanas
        not as good-looking
                as a racehorse,

but look as if they know
        how to stand
                their ground.

Wreckage

There was a warning before it arrived,
        the sound of a road train dismantling,
                the second time it was the shatter of metal

dragged on asphalt, a plane's unsuccessful landing,
        and going to the kitchen saw her at the window.
                The sound may have been compulsive sobs

or the coughing up of bone stuck in her throat
        but no one else seemed to hear:
                my father at the table reading the *The Age*,

my sisters running around the house,
        my brother hitting a ball against a wall.
                A silent house to the unobserved wreckage.

Statistically

1

Consider the speed of the bullet.
Slow it down so you witness its movement
like in time-slice photography, and you see
the small missile that it is, before it hits
and separates flesh. Depending on where
it hits decides whether you die or lay
maimed. Sometimes you are saved by a millimetre,
sometimes by the angle it enters. Sometimes
you are lucky, as if the angle is your angel.

2

Bullet, from the French *boulle*, meaning
'small ball', sweet and innocuous
as a school dance. They come in all sizes,
expressed by weight and diameter.
There are the common .22 and .303,
up to the .95 calibre.
Bullets travel at 343 metres per second
with slight modifications for air temperature
and dew levels. The target can almost be
dead before you hear the bang.

3

Bullets need guns.
Their availability varies. In the US
you can buy one at your local Walmart.
Other countries are harder. There are handguns,
assault rifles, sniper guns, semi-automatic
shotguns. In Africa, AK-47s
or Kalashnikovs are preferred,
carried by child soldiers only twice their size.

4

Guns need people. Guns are not dangerous,
people are, is the truism. That's why
they shouldn't be available.

In 2015, there were 372 mass shootings
and 33,636 deaths due to firearms
in the US. More people are killed in a day
in the US than the UK in a year.

A seemingly ordinary man in Las Vegas
found himself an apartment and filled
it with guns and waited for the last song
as he looked out on the concert below.

Eighty-five people die a day from guns
in the United States. Fifty-nine more
hardly shifts the weekly average.

Look! Old People

Look! Old people. Waiting the crosswalk,
hesitant in their first steps like children,
looking both ways again just in case.
There's another one, trying to get upstairs,
they shouldn't be out in public spaces
scaring us with our future selves,
meeting us unexpectedly with frail steps
and faltering minds. They should come
with warnings. There is no need to be out
so often. The women wear too much perfume,
the men's pants far too high. They have everything
at home, shopping centres deliver, there is no need…
perhaps cloaking technology will find ways to mask
their appearance, make them invisible,
give warnings of their whereabouts.
We who have spent so much on exercise,
miracle diets, skin treatments and surgery.
Look! There's more – a group of them on the beach
in bathers! Joking and laughing as if they were kids.

The Film Version of the Poet's Life

In the film version of my life – a blockbuster in the megaplexes –
I will appear the working class boy facing adversity
who becomes the poet. Years of rejections and disappointments,
till finally a major prize. My work is then reassessed,
(all in a one minute montage) but still I am tormented,
carrying an emptiness that must be visible,
and which I must discover – it is for this that I write.
Dozens of temporary loves till finally a woman –
down to earth and not a writer, yet sensitive & intuitive –
takes me in hand. We leave the city and find authenticity.
Have children late in life, all giving new direction for my poetry.
The last shot has me on a beach looking out to sea,
music that captures epiphany and quick shot to children building
    sandcastles.

In the Indie version I face adversity, disappointment and anomie,
and never get over it. Film noir with lots of shots at night,
    flashbacks
sepia & grainy. Night bars, drunkenness, finding myself
    committing lewd acts
with women of all ages, usually against walls. I scrawl poems on
    bits of paper,
only get published after drowning while on a beachside bender.

Eve : ning

We had been travelling all day,
the conversation cursory,
the distance between us intact.

We crossed no border, no lines
marked our exit, no gate
our exile, but we knew

when we passed. He quickly looked back,
like he is meant to, or perhaps
expecting to see himself left behind.

It was an animal track, grown
over in parts. We kept moving,
learning wariness, learning danger

in every sound. We found a new tongue
of curses for the insects that bit,
the heat as it rose, the cold as it fell.

It was night we feared,
when it came we were shocked
and touched one another other
for the first time that day.

Around us darkness callused
its completion, allowing
no residual light to tell us
where we had arrived.

Perth

Perth is as far away from Manhattan
as is airlinely possible.
The sky is always blue.
We have beaches as long as Thai surnames.
It is the last stop before
it is shorter to travel the other way.
We talk about the weather a lot,
know many synonyms for blue.
Cobalt. Azure. Cerulean.

Anyway, Manhattan has no beaches.
New Yorkers have to travel hours
to Long Island, bustle their way to the Hamptons
for tepid water.
(Did I tell you how cerulean our sky is?)
So what if you can see Al Pacino
play *Shylock in the Park*,
see the latest plays by Shepard and Mamet,
stand next to ancient Egypt rebuilt in the Met.
So! There are too many sirens at night.
Too much energy. Too many people
wanting to go somewhere.
And even if they have newspapers that do massive
Arts spreads, have the *New Yorker*,
and bookshops you can get lost in
(OK I love those moveable ladders that slide across a room),
the subway is too hot, the weather
too humid in summer, too cold in winter.

If aliens came to Earth
they would never raise their kids in Manhattan.
No way. They'd set up house on the beaches
of Perth, or head south to the beaches and vineyards,
and yes you can buy Australian wine for half the price
in New York, but there is just too much choice.
The aliens would stash their spacecraft,
sit on the front porch overlooking the ocean
staring up at the cobalt sky, thinking of home.

Font

The first rain after a dry summer
gives the world a delineated edge,
darker and striking, like changing
fonts: Times Roman to Arial.

The same happens after not seeing you
for months; you appear by accident
sans serif, easier to read in sunlight.

Walled Cities

I'd like to live within a walled city,
with all the barbarians kept beyond.
All the things you need in walking
distance. The streets narrow and winding,
leading to the city square: the church
at one end, city hall the other. Women
in high heels adept at treading the pebbled
paths, cats content with sardines in their mouths.
There would be music in the square each night
and cafés with talk of philosophers and poets.
On still nights you can sit on the ramparts,
hear the raucous ramblings of the rabble,
smell the animal fat roasting on fires,
and listen to threats in the distant babble.

Distance and Mrs Cook

Captain, your wife is waiting,
waiting in a town smelling
of tanneries and breweries,
of rope and death.

Remember that young Banks arriving
at Plymouth? You didn't know the Admiralty
had given him a special berth, they didn't
bother to tell you, the ship's captain,
that he was sailing to Tahiti, till he strolled
down the dock, two African servants
and two greyhounds in hand. He was as rich
as Lucullus, came from the landed gentry
but you didn't mind. After the aristocrats
that had snubbed you, he was all cheer and good humour,
never pulled rank, never needed
to display his birthright.

Your wife is waiting.
Twelve years in fifteen you have been away.
She awaits your return,
awaits another child in her womb.

You knew where you came from,
knew your place, knew only the sea
could change it, so you left the village
where you would have become your father,
found the mathematics that would save you
and calculated your escape.

Your wife is still waiting. This was the trip
that would etch your name in stars. No one
could read the oceans like you, navigate
and calculate the earth and sky like you.
No one believed as you that the world
could be measured. Humourless perhaps,
too serious to have friends, you made
yourself irreplaceable.

There were times you couldn't believe
your luck, couldn't believe how numbers
and trigonometry had made the world
so ordered. How mathematicians
had conjured perfect lines from chaos.
You would sway and feel seasick till you
closed your eyes and waited for it to pass.

Your wife is waiting
waiting with her dead children.
You lost all four siblings when young,
now your children are dying. You know
about death as every captain should.
Twenty-eight crew died on your first trip.
No ship ever returned without death stationed
on every deck. But your children are dying
and you are oceans away.

Men will always die. It is what God decreed.
Men will always die on tiny boats on oceans,
chartered or not, where there is nothing to save
them except a god and a good captain,
and better still when they're one person,
so you kept an omniscient distance.
Your wife will outlive all her children and you.
Well into her eighties she will be waiting at her door
an old straw broom in hand poking young death
in the ribs, muttering she had grown old around him.

Jellyfish

The box jellyfish, *Chironex fleckeri*
can kill you in four minutes. Its transparent
box head trails a bridal veil of tentacles
tipped with tiny hypodermics, a spiked kiss
that deters any weary consumption.
The Irukandji will make you want to die
without leaving a mark. The pain begins
with cramps up your spine. It is like being
throttled by a crazed midnight lout with a steel
bar. Your blood shakes through you in breathless
spasms and your skin inhabited by wriggling
maggots that become spiders. This is payback:
for once having the open oceans to themselves,
for the conceit of late-comers crawling to land.

Small Detonations

i.m. Barrie Wells

There are hundreds of footprints, small detonations
marking the weight of the human body,
left in the soft sand after the weekend.
They vary in depth from the curvature
of foot, the speed that it touched surface.
Barrie lived in Margaret Street and jogged
from Grant to the Cott groyne for years, pressing
his weight into soft sand, making a presence
that came from a gravity that relentlessly
keeps us at ground level. Nearer to the edge,
where ocean meets land, where sand hardens,
the prints disappear as if we have all
become weightless, disappearing completely
as we leave earth into an expanse of fluidity.

Elephants

The elephants were sad and grey in their hard
creases, so I let them out. There was no one
to stop me so I just opened the gate,

told them to run, scat, be free.
Told them this was their big chance.
I didn't intend the damages, the casualties.

Perhaps I could have done it with greater order:
tied them together and taken them for a walk,
leashed and scolded like young, boisterous children,

or shown them the sights like tourists,
walk them to the ocean – show them infinity
and return them to walls, walls, walls.

Or perhaps I could have climbed aboard like a mahout,
with their tails and trunks joined, parade
them around the city, to the amazement of crowds.

Elephants kill more humans than most
of the great predators on the savannah.
The great cats evolved to kill and sleep,

but elephants you trust in their mawkish
awkwardness. Despite their weight,
great tusks and unexpected speed.

There are no cliffs where lemmings leap, no
graveyards for elephants, no God to die for.

Angle

I only knew an angle of my father. An acute angle. A tiny slice that changed from where you stood. I sometimes caught him in the corner of my eye and thought that's him. Getting out of his truck, dirty from work, pine resin on his arm hair, black oil across his face. Or in the Chrysler with the kids singing.

Never was.

I tried to look in the wrong direction, hoping he had left something of himself. Just a trace, so had I been a sniffer-dog I could have tracked him.

But he was light-footed, shadowless.

He came home everyday but was never there, came home everyday with his one trick of disappearing into light.

Beachfront

The first thing God created was the journey, then came doubt, and nostalgia… – Theo Angelopoulos

1. Journey

They are throwing a ball. A father and his two
girls. Perhaps thirteen and seventeen, too old
to bother with fathers, but here they are,
throwing an old tennis ball, leaping
and screaming themselves around the ocean.
In the middle of winter, in stark July cold,
they are throwing themselves into waves, throwing
a ball and watching the parabola
of flight as it lands in another's hands. Two
daughters with their dad, coming down to the beach.
You can hear their joy, the shrieks and screams.
A parabola of flight, an old ball and laughter.
A dad and his girls catching waves, catching flight,
coordinated movements keeping them tight.

2. Doubt

The mother is holding hands with her daughter,
looking out to sea through a circle of sculpture.
From this angle it looks as if she is in the shooter's
lens. First there are the young men surfing
on the reef, the swell undulated like a sine curve,
further out men fishing in tinnies, in the backdrop
the cargo ships facing south though there is no wind,
waiting in Gage Road. There is an island beyond
but today it is grey cliffs that are not really there.
Beyond is what interests the mother:
she knows there is ocean all the way to another
continent. Out there is a hundred ways to die,
a hundred ways to live. If only I could give
up land, she thinks, as if land were grief
she injected. Her daughter's gaze is fixed
firmly on the young boys on the reef

3. Nostalgia

There was an old deli on Avonmore,
a corner store with a little bottle shop
on the side, where the owner would drag
out forgotten boxes of wine, holding
a bottle like a chalice. There were ropes and tyres
on the pylon, before they re-built
the stem as a pointed missile pre-empting
all leaps of frivolity. The old garage
on Eric Street where men in overalls
talked and joked while pouring petrol.
The Eats van on the coast, the flour
mill that is now exclusive apartments.
The beachfront they are coming for: the movers,
gigantic hoovers, sucking back the firmament.

Spelling

Dear Mr Maroney, you probably don't remember me, unless through my absences. At a recent reunion we decided to form a group to talk out our schooldays. Teachers that were a distinct influence. Marked our way through life. Your name came up first – quite vehemently in fact – especially when we recalled how you lined us around the wall for spelling. A bit like being on the other side of the firing squad. You using words like bullets. Answers quick and unfaltering, or else to the back of the line. At the end of the lesson the last five boys were strapped. Laurie O'Neill – the red head you called Blue – still can't line up in queues unless there are five people behind him. He's had a life of being abused or shoved to the back. Mick Taylor never had a stuttering problem till he couldn't get out sustenance right before the bell. The perfect student who got strapped. You told him it would keep him on his toes. Den Rand hates his kids asking him how to spell a word. You kept the strap on the desk or sometimes in your back pocket. It looked like a small black tail and with your wrinkled face gave us one of your nicknames, monkey Maroney. Chris Hill still has an unnatural aversion to the lesser apes and some of the smaller tailed primates. But it was the threat of your special strap, Jumbo, you called it, speaking affectionately of it as if it was your cat or dog. The way you soaked it in oil once a month to give it flex or polished it with boot polish to keep its shine. It was hidden in a back cupboard that you kept locked. We could only remember you using it once (on Phil Ray – typical) but the fear of it kept us wary. Sam Locke had to sit next to it at the back of the room. We were seated from one at the front to forty-eight at the back dependent on our tests. His analyst attributes most of his neuroses to the palpable presence of Jumbo – alive and breathing, oiled like a body-builder in the darkness of the cupboard. You took most of our meeting, you and your spelling line and the oiled Jumbo. Steve Gatt reminded us how you would trick us into learning our lists by asking the compound word in the list or the word that rhymes with. He said you had little effect on him and had come along for the alcohol but he did say that he remembers you when he hears the compound-word that double-rhymes with pass and role.

Square of Yellow Light

I came home late one night, very late,
to find my father making his lunch
in the square of yellow light in the kitchen.
We stared each other down. He standing
at the bench cutting thick slabs of bread,
filling the holes of day with processed cheese.
I thought it was resentment that stared out
at me from behind the bench. His nineteen-
year-old son at university coming home
early morning, having climbed out of some
girl's bed. A boy who had never done a hard
day's work. He could only see me as frivolous.
Then he asked if I wanted a cuppa tea,
and there may have been admiration,
some eye contact of approval as he looked up.
I said, What's wrong, but he smiled and remarked,
I was the clever one, I should know.
But I was never that smart.

Your Wanderings

Your wanderings have become rare. There's been
sightings and I map the stars for your location.
The nights are light, days darken. There have been
sightings. There are obstacles in place;
geographically fixed. We had slipped around
them on high tides, hardly noticing
their solidity beneath surface, now you
keep to land. I can see you across the strait,
sometimes you wave. Your wanderings have become rare.
The meteorologist says there are storms
forecasted over our heads. The diviner
has thrown the bones and tells us that we shall
be lost before we are found, I write messages on walls
of cafés, footpaths, the hulls of boats: come, urgent.

Chance

They blame me though I never had a chance. Take responsibility, son. You have as much chance as the next man, but I know it's not true for any of us. The old man never had a chance as he sat glued to the news. Still he goes on. Responsibility. Choice. The poor bastard had his wires chewed through by rats. They tell you you're free, free to be who you will, then tell you to dance straight, keep that tie subdued and to the collar. Show respect to your betters, though they're the same feckers doing us over. It's a nasty circle, I told him once. Wanted to say how many times have you gone wrong, Dad? Ever likely to change the way it is? The brains you were born with, the parents who did their best, though we know that means useless. The school you went to, the kids you hung with, the way you spoke, the thousand little things that happened as a kid, most you didn't recognise, that made you who you were, made you go one way and not another. Persistence. Determination. Is all they say, as if I was taught or born with the same sizeable allocation. That's all you need my mum joins in, though I know she read it in a mag. I tell her, yeah Mum, like getting dropped way out in the Tanami Desert and told to get to the coast in our bare feet and no water, while others get a Range Rover stacked with food for the trip. Stopping for picnics on the way. She didn't like that, didn't know where I got these twisted thoughts. You don't have a leftie teacher, do you? I'll ring that school of yours, though she's too scared to say a word to people behind a desk in a spin-chair. Well where did you get all that stuff you believe? Come down from high on a ray of sunlight. Don't you blaspheme, my boy. You show your mother a bit of respect and the God that made you. But he didn't, you did Mum, and your mum had it off with your father to get you, and on and on. I want to tell her to take responsibility but there's a line. You're going straight to hell, though I did my best. The best you could Mum, and I don't blame you for it. I'll get your father she threatens, but he's having a beer and not interested in stuff like this, and I don't blame him, I don't hold him responsible. It's OK I want to say. You're no more to blame than the dark cloud's downpour of rain, the shark's unceasing movement, the wave for breaking on shallow reef. Nor are you to be congratulated.

Avocado

1

it is morning
beneath the shade
of leaves
as i
watch
avocados hanging green
like carved omens

choosing one
from a low branch
i
slice
it in halves

digging out its
brown-seed soul
and waited
to eat
its pale sunset
of flesh

2

The morning always comes again,
parting the flesh of day,

letting fall its head
between the knees of noon.

3

in a past
a boy
still young enough

brought home
an avocado-seed
polished and opal-brown

it may have
been cared for
by some motherly
deviant-of-pearl
keeping it these years
for him

he kissed it
into soil
and waited for

stem
leaf
sigh
to appear

he grafted
with
sexless gasps

and waited
for
fruit

for
seven years
he waited

till the
first avocado
appeared

hanging
like a carved omen.

Moorings

With eye
with tongue
have I known you

With scorpion
have you
filled my head

Night rings
its dreadful
note

I hear the wind-strewn,
sea-brewed wilderness
wash itself upon the beach

Leaving its message
scribbled in weed

Cows

On the road to Balangan
amidst the deft movement
of bodies & motorbikes

the smells of fermenting fruit & exhaust
a wondrous makeshift world
that slides between centuries

is a woman nursing a young child
beneath the shade of a *waru*
surrounded by cows

A young mother
aware of the cool serenity
of being encircled by cows

The Bones of a Tiger

I

There were fifteen tigers left
in the forests of Ranthambor,
fourteen now since a man was caught
stealing out from a poacher's track.
There were traces of flesh
glued to the still warm bones,
the joints like large fists
that had hours before sculptured
his soft movements beneath banyan trees.

There is a market for such things:
it is said the drinker's body
harden with the animal
that had dragged down oxen and cows,
giving back the lithe
and marriages are said to have improved.

II

I once saw a Bengali tiger
in a Chinese zoo.
I had never imagined their full size,
its weight killing you
before its jaws ripped away your throat.

I had to step backwards till
I was almost in a pool of lilies
before I could capture him on film.
The dark bars of cage losing themselves
on the tiger's symmetry of stripes.

I have the photograph behind plastic,
just in case.
He has turned his head,
eyeing, from the corner of his cage
my fleshed bones,
on the opposite side of the album.

Age Takes a Socialist

I thought every family had one, but kids
at school never mentioned a socialist aunt
and uncle. Ours drove a Holden FJ,
the people's car, went to city meetings
and gave out yellowing pamphlets. When they grew
older they went through a phase where they talked
constantly of their preferred deaths. They refused
to reach seventy, wanted a quiet bed-death,
though they had never been quiet all their lives,
an aneurysm or heart attack might do,
but there would be no nursing home, never
that dilution. Their lives had been a fight
against institutions. Euthanasia
became an obsession. They spoke of Death
as a greedy capitalist with a monopoly
in the futures market, and they were at
the battlements again, proclaiming
their rights, their ownership of death.
Then it passed, some small shift in the brain,
and getting up and having a cup of tea was enough,
it was one-thing-at-a-time; the revolution
subsided. My uncle would have shouted
and raved at this diminished self, this
broken man who was not him, had he
a mind to think it through. His death
by dementia orchestrated by secret
cabals. Aunt lived on for years in a nursing
home, watching TV game shows with a boyfriend.

Wagtail

The wagtail doesn't know it is small.
It has evolved to believe it is five times
its size. Smug as a wall, quick as a fall.
A stand-up comic to the humourless crow,
who it chases and berates for it slowwittedness.
It teases the cat, darting
away at the last moment, swooping
and fluttering above, the way fairies
do in old movies. When the doors are closed
it boasts at the glass, flipping it great tail
like a tiny conductor in a tux, dancing
to the cat's chagrin on the other side.
It is too big to realise how many creatures
would like to hear the snap of its small bones.
would like the taste of its smart-arse blood.

Finnegan Goes to War

This is our own peninsula war. Lord
Kirkmount – make a mountain out of a hill,
a cathedral out of a chapel – said
it'd take quite a few men to take the Straits
but we'd be rid of the Heathens. Then take
the beach – camesawconquered – with boys who knew
beaches. The commanders all British and Sirs.
This is our hill to get up. This is our enemy
to shoot. But it looks like home: same trees, smells, white sand.
We're off to Achi Baba said a hyphenated-
General Sir. We light cigarettes and hope for Christmas,
but the Damntohelles is mined and the ships
can't get through and we're told what to do by prats
in big hats who never been east of Corfu.

Number 7

He lived alone in Number 7, his wife well gone. He slept in the afternoons, woke in the middle of the night and went to the kitchen to make a cup of tea and smoke a cigarette. He only smoked one a day and looked forward to it.

Number 7 was the worse house in the street.

He often sat in a plastic chair on the front porch and watched the kids coming home from school. He rode a green scooter, a lime-green scooter, the type that has trouble getting up steep hills.

Sometimes he played old cassettes and cried. When it became too much he went into the garden and pruned the plumbago into a perfect sphere. Pruned the hedge into a triangle.

They use to picnic on the lawn. On hot nights they spread a blanket and ate chicken and drank red wine.

The body and blood. Amen.

The Five Ages

1

As kids we ran with wild nor-westers,
arms out as if we could fly,
screaming into the wind.

Never forgetting the smell: sea-brewed,
weed-strewn, wild sea-herbs mixed
by wind conjurors, who may have been gods.

We heard the voice of the wind and threw
ourselves into the ocean, hurled ourselves
across waves, unable to imagine tomorrow.

2

there goes adolescence with its dreadful lies of permanence,
some catholic limbo without blame or reward,
the border zone where you try your ID and passwords
that allow you back but the guardians, adult and dull,
calm and unperturbed, with brutal smiles like razor wire,
lift the gate and usher you in, bemused by those hanging
back, imagining they can't be seen – convinced
they can contrive their way back when night falls.

3

That once was me, young and bohemian.
With a beret slouched aggressively,
a roll-your-own in my hand, on a jetty
under the light. Happens to all of us:
quondam: I of previous days of my
former identity am no longer available –
no access to, no forwarding email, no tweet account.
I who was me yesterday is no longer he.
Took a wrong turn and slipped the ecliptic
and am now tracing the fall.

4

It is more the fanfare than the funfair when you get old
we think we're here for the funfair till it turns a little feral
chasing the rides up and down and up and down
the wild mouse and slippery dip the yelling yellowing
adrenalin alleyways music pulsating against the wall
or backofthecar and you both light a cig and it's good
most of the time though not really funferallthetime
and fanfares start to make sense – time to lay foundations,
make others notice otherwise there'll never be a fanfare –
so you hide that feral self good and tight
tied & leashed to keep it from running away with the circus.

5

Solstice of stilling
  where a planet hangs
    at its furthest edge

    in stillbirth silence
  some solar clock tracks us down
like fleeing future-tives

dragging another year from us
  its lens never lingering
    on stillness, or the illness

    that encroaches
  the unspoken that nears each day
that old skateboard run

the hill we'd thrill down
in the middle of the night
when the hours did not count

Interstices

My mother liked words,
she would say, 'In the interstices
between the beginning and the end,
between my husband leaving for war,
and returning cigarette-thin,
between taking me to live in the bush
in an army tent, and the first child,
between waking with an eye out for dugites
and cooking dinner in a wood stove,
in between, in the interstices,
I dreamed of the sea.'

www.ingramcontent.com/pod-product-compliance
Lightning Source LLC
Chambersburg PA
CBHW062201100526
44589CB00014B/1898